Trichotomy : this is me

TRICHOTOMY : this is me

by Esskei

Hevhanli Soul
Toronto

Trichotomy : this is me
Copyright © 2009 by Esskei. All rights reserved. No part of this book may be used or reproduced in any manner whatsoever without written permission except in the case of brief quotations embodied in critical articles or reviews. For information, address Hevhanli Soul, (insert address).

www.hevhanlisoul.com

Cover Design by Koree Haye of Gadget Graphics
Book Design by Hevhanli Soul

National Library of Canada Cataloguing-in-Publication Data

Esskei, 1979-
    Trichotomy : this is me. - 1st ed.
   p.cm.
   ISBN 978-0-9812436-1-0

First Edition May, 2010

Definition

Trichotomy [tri-kot-uh-mee]: 1. division into three parts, classes, categories. etc., 2. an instance of such a divison, as in thought, structure, or object., 3. the three-part divison of human beings into body, spirit, and soul.

Table of Contents

Introduction   xv

Soma

20 Feelings   1
I Know…?   2
Untitled #12   3
The Symphony   4
Stage 5   6
My Name Is   7
Mom'ma Rose   8
Hungry 4 Knowledge   9
Milk's Secret   10
Lovejonse   11
Caught by the Fire in Your Eyes   13
P.M.   14
Imperfections   16
Constant Attraction   17
Ebony Kingdom (conception seq #1)   18
Untitled #72   19
In Love With Yourself or the Possiblity?   20
Devol   21
The Cee-lo Green Mentality   22
The Bloody Page   23
I Almost Let Go   24
Your Beauty Reminds Me of   25
Rain on Me   26
Spoke w/ Tongues   27
Neo Expression   29

Psyche

Selfish　33
I Have a Dream Too　34
That Only Leaves 3　36
Hard to Know　37
5th Element of Hip Hop　38
Artistry　39
Could That Be Me?　40
Disrupted　41
I Am a Black Man　43
I Don't Know What It's Like　44
Emptiness (Death Part 1)　46
Against the System　47
Inter-Dimensional Consciousness　49
Money Not Sense Controls Individual Intent　50
New Revolutionary　51
Not a Conversationalist　52
S-5-N　53
Public Transpo　54
Not Slaves, But Sons　56
Stand Against Webster's　57
The Girl Next Door　59
Viagra　60
Ying Ying　61
Good-bye Faye　62
Labels　63
Openly　64
Starving Art Is (starving artist)　66
Youngsters Façade　69

Pneuma

Dinner Skipped Me　74
Substitue Teacher　75
As I Pray　76
Classic Salvation Sauce　77
Forced 2 Focus　78
God 4 Give　80

Hook: Change Bridge: Mentality Verse: Sin   **81**
I Still Am   **83**
Love @ Birth   **84**
SHE Wondered   **85**
Our Vow   **87**
So That I See You Tomorrow   **88**
Time   **90**
Thinking of You   **91**
A New Moon   **92**
The Road to Peter   **96**
Knocks Deception   **98**
Crucified   **99**
This Year Christmas Made Me Nervous   **101**

Bonus Poem (This is ME!)   **106**

Lists of Illustrations

Esskei's artwork and graphic design appears on pp. 5, 12, 28, 65, 68, 78, 95
Web site www.HEVHANLISOUL.com
Contact info: esskeimusic@gmail.com

Smile of lil *D* on pp. 103 taken by *Proud Mommy*

Awaovieyi's artwork appears on pp. 95 and chapter title pages
Contact info: awaovieyi@hotmail.com

Koree Haye's of Gadget Graphics photograph of Esskei on pp. 82
Contact info: contact@gadgetgraphics.ca

Colleen Paul's of BFX Photography photograph of Esskei on pp. 78
Web site www.BFXPHOTOGRAPHY.com
Contact info: butterfly_fx_04@hotmail.com

JaNae Armogan's photograph of *"Cherish"* Esskei on piano on pp. 5
Web site www.JANAEARMOGAN.com

Family photographys taken by *random family* on pp. 21, 22, 28, 35, 42, 48, 52, 58, 73, 84, 89

David Screaming on pp. 68 by *Judith Shelke*

I've gotten lost in my dreams. You've helped me find me.

Thnx U
- Esskei

Introduction

First I got to say God, this has been a long time coming and I thank you for the journey. Second, I would like to thank everyone who has purchased, borrowed or read this book. You have made a difference in my life and I hope that this book has made a difference in yours. Fists up, feet on the ground!

Over the years I have fought within myself about exactly who I am and about what my purpose in life is and eventually where it would take me. Not knowing where you fit into society can be a weird and awkward place, but I know we have all at some point been there. Simply because we all want to leave our mark on this world. We want our family and loved ones to say, "Look at what my son Darrius has accomplished" or "Did you know that my niece Jonelle is the fastest junior sprinter in Ontario? I'm so proud of her." These are things we want our loved ones to say about us - or to us at some point in our life. It provides a sense of satisfaction to our ego, and allows us to feel justified within ourselves as we fight to truly understand who we are.

So who am I? This is something I am still sorting out. But believe me when I tell you, I am more comfortable with myself now at this point of the journey than I was at the beginning. I was born in Calgary and started to write as a way to escape from my inner thoughts. I was in a place where red was no longer a colour and fish couldn't swim, but still had a place in the water. I felt as though my inner thoughts and self-loathing were inescapable. Can you imagine living in a place where creativity is not nurtured? Where creativity is stifled? Do you see it? If so, welcome to my world.

My earliest memory of writing is at the age of six or seven. I was really upset after our first move to Toronto. I remember the day exactly. We came home from school to a completely empty house, our mother waiting at the front door and our bags in the van ready to go. There was no warning, and no understanding as to why. I couldn't figure it out then and honestly I really don't get it now. All I know is that I didn't want to be at home anymore, so I made up a story about being alone on an adventure. "The Search for the Golden Eagle", that was my first piece of work. I later threw it out. I didn't want my family to get a hold of it and read it. I felt that someone would insult it, and make fun of me. So the trend began. I wrote and destroyed my work. My ego wouldn't allow the opportunity for someone to kill my therapy the way they did my love for drawing years earlier. Everyone in my house could see me when I'd draw. I never hid it. I started out tracing comic book characters, and then I taught myself to look at the comic and draw it till it was perfect. I mastered shading, colouring and before long I even mastered my own technique. But I was a budding flower of art that was at times being over watered or not watered at all. After a move back and forth from Calgary to Toronto to Calgary and then back to Toronto my artistic flower was over watered and died. Writing was still my best kept secret.

  Even though I did not want to share my writing with anyone, I needed someone to say, "look at David… isn't he talented!" Sadly my ego showed up when they killed the love I had for drawing. The only option was to put my writing out there. So less and less poems were thrown out. This was around the time I started making birthday cards for my mother and father as gifts and poems dedicated to those who asked for a poem. It seems like everyone wants a poem when they find out that you write poetry, but I guess the same is true when they find out you have any talent. I remember I was writing a few poems at a time every day until one day I just stopped. I was tired. My thoughts seemed to clump together as one and no one poem seemed different than the other. Growing up will do that to your passion sometimes. You lose yourself as you grow, I guess only to hopefully find yourself again. Well I was still searching, but still felt as if I made a mistake in sharing this gift as I did my love for drawing.

  In "Could that be her?" I explored the possibility of love as I observe a couple expressing their love, imagining that I am him. As I looked deeper into myself, I realized that I'd been substituting myself for most of my life. Trying to replace every aspect of my life that I felt was unsatisfactory. The day dreaming began.a Over time I lost more and more of my ego started to gain a hold over the purity of who I truly was and somewhere down the line I became self-centered and egotistical.

By this time I was about 19yrs old. I had just moved back Brampton from Edmonton after attending school and again was home with the family. Although the dynamics of my family had changed, the actual structure was really the same. My father had left for good this time. This would start a 7-year silence on my part when it came to my father. The house was still full of brotherly arguments, laughter, girls coming by, the guys playing basketball or football out on the street. There was never a dull moment on Blackmere Circle. There was always something to do, so that's exactly what I did. From drinking, hanging, partying, fighting, working and when I was not doing that I was at church. I was still trying to find myself, and church played a major role in who I became but so did the drinking, partying and so on. It was my new public release. Were they all good options, I can't say that they were but they were options nonetheless.

During this time I started to think of business ideas; starting with selling gospel CD's and other Christian based merchandise. However, that went nowhere fast. I had everything lined up perfectly and even had a partner. Things just didn't work out, Lighthouse Music was unsuccessful. But the drive to be my own boss didn't end there. I added a few more partners and tried to start an umbrella corporation that housed a fashion line, graphic design business, record company, and a marketing firm. However, due to different personal relationships coming to an end Intouch Foundations never saw the light of day. To this day I still look at the business plan we developed and am only now seeing companies following our ideal format for business success. So by the time I was 22yrs old I was involved with 2 companies that didn't even get out of the intro stage of the business life cycle. Let's just say that my level of confidence was almost none existent, and through this time my writing started to be more consistent and it was here I really decided to put out my own book of poetry.

Through years of research, I learned what it would take to get my book published and it started to kill my desire. After realizing that most publishing companies only publish 1-2 poetry books a year I felt that my chances were very slim. I looked into self-publishing with different publishing companies, but the costs to do so were different and I didn't know exactly what I would be willing to pay for, so I kept researching.

The bible talks about being equally yoked and I've always thought it meant spiritually equal. Completely ignoring the other aspects of being a human being living on this beautiful planet our creator made for us. At this time I was just fired from Telus and decided to take this time to get away for awhile. I decided that now was the time to lock my hair. This is when I met Kaysee. She is the most beautiful spirit that I have ever met. After going to South Carolina and visiting my spiritual father Apostle Clark for a few months I came back with a different focus, I started to slow down on the partying, the drinking, and the desire to fill a void of release with simply doing things 'just because'. I came back and Kaysee helped me realize that I needed to be more than who I was turning out to be. I started to perform and really work on my poetry. By this time I was soon to be a father and my life had changed dramatically. My family dynamic had seriously changed. I was now a dad, I started speaking to my father, but I stopped speaking with my mother and ended ties with my oldest brother. New life is a mysterious event that affects all around it. Some react positively and see the blessings the new life has brought into their lives, while others see this new life as a negative and react that way. I guess they felt the birth of my son was negative, because ever since he was born they have yet to see what a blessing he is. So it feels like I'm in a coma and I can't see or hear them around me. Mainly because they're not and this coma has allowed me time to realize a lot about myself and recognize that things had to change.

Kaysee not liking the change she saw in me put me onto reading more. She gave me "Do You" by Russell Simmons and "The Measure of a Man: A Spiritual Autobiography" by Sydney Poitier. After reading these books I realized even more so that everyone who has achieved some sort of success has done so through sacrifice. Now I'm not saying that separating from family is a sacrifice because sometimes it feels that way. But it is a hardship most aren't willing to go through. I decided that my life was worth more than unwanted arguments and a false sense of trust. However, I still wasn't sure where I belonged. So I decided to read "A New Earth" by Eckhart Tolle. This is where I realized that everything I was feeling towards my family was my ego and I needed to learn to separate myself from my ego and really look at that situation. I'm happy to say I'm still looking.

Now, still trying to find out who I am and battle against my ego, I am in control of my pride even though I was a very proud individual. My ego didn't stop me from asking those who were successful within my genre and industry, how they got to where they are now? What mistakes they've made? So I swallowed my pride knowing that I couldn't do it alone. Dwayne Morgan was a great help asking the questions that I was too afraid to ask myself but were necessary. Karen Richardson has been a big supporter and connected me with Kevin 'Heron' Jones, Kevin was happy to edit my book and inspired me with his feedback. It was after connecting with Dwayne, Karen poetically and Kevin that I started to surround myself with people who were following the same path. I needed to be everything my book was about and less of a one-dimensional or two-dimensional person. . I needed to be a three dimensional person who is more than just pride or ego, a person who is connected, physically, mentally and spiritually to this earth and the people within it.

Trichotomy : this is me is that connection to the earth and all the people within it. These poems have taught me how to really examine the person that I was and the person I dreamed about being. The person I've been replacing with someone else since I was six or seven years old, the same person that I almost lost. I hope that if you've lost yourself, that after examining this book, you will rediscover who you really are. I know I have.

Esskei

SOMA

Sight

Touch

Smell

Taste

Sound

20 Feelings

Memories of satisfied feelings
Overshadowed feelings
Other feelings
:Misleading feelings
Right feelings
Wrong feelings
Wrong feelings that I thought were right feelings
Blowing up in my face feelings
Feelings that made my heart jump
You know breath stopping feelings
Vein popping, frustrated by these feelings
Laughing, just trying to get over those feelings
Or else they'll turn into 911 type feelings
But I love you, so I stay away from those feelings
This is funny because I never gave into feelings
But since feeling you
That's all I can feel, are my feelings
My feelings for you
You are why I feel
And it feels amazing, this feeling

I Know You...?

I know you
By your smell
The scent of passion
And beauty that fills the air
As you enter and leave again
And again

I know you
By the movement of your body
As you move
The shape of your body
Is spelled out through your grace

I recognize you
By your voice
The sound of a sweet
Soft voice speaking words of love and encouragement

I recognize you
By your beauty
Every bit of you
Uniquely different
As I stare into your eyes
I see something new every time

We act as if we have known each other for a long time
When really we've only met a few times

Can I get to know you deeper than this?
Can I see you?
Greet you with a kiss
I need to know you
Can I know you?

Untitled #12

I placed myself on the line

I should have waited before I told you
How could I not express myself to you the way I truly know how to

So I gave you emotions on a page
Not once but twice within a few days
Maybe it should have been once
But the thought of you got me going on this day
Listening to a jazzy vibe
Of love and ecstasy
My mind began to look and found the one I could love
My mind found you
So I began to write
Then sent letters to you
The fastest way I knew how
Now I wait to see
The response you'll give to me
If you respond to it at all
But I will ask you through words
Face-to-face
Before this month is through
When I see the beauty which is you

The Symphony

Soft to the touch
My fingers slide along your gentle ebony complexion
Playing a melody of temptation
I desire to sit
Cool and calm
Your underlying frustrations
With chords of love tuned into octaves of steaming lust
Every note
Changes the focus of my purpose
Pleasing you as I play
Tenderly to your every need
Surrounded by candles and black noir incense
Radiantly engulf the room as my hands begin to strike each chord
Note
Prompting you to sing that high soprano
"Ohhh, Ohhh, GO……..O"
Unable to finish your song
Improvisations bridge the gap
Of chorus and verse
As the tone for ecstasy is set
Waiting for you
I s the tender tip of my forbidden kiss
Wrapped firmly around your lips
As we play soulfully with each other
The ebony on the piano
Until climax at the bridge
When a soft drip of ivory becomes played with my fingers, touching gently every nerve
Rushing through your silky ebony body
The chords vibrate and shake in your ebony piano case
The grand piano opens
As I play strings rubbing
Between chords
Echoing while you sing
I play as you lay in measure
While I compose and arrange you
To my pleasure

Stage 5

To come home to you!
I remember clearly how I felt when I spoke to you
The way my heart melts as I listen to you
How my body moved after staring in your eyes
I longed to speak to you, and be part of your life
Things moved so smoothly within the time since we met
We went from speaking in person
Face-to-face
This was the first stage from the first day
I said yep
Then moving all over the town, you and I grew
To know each other as your family showed me around
That night I spent it knowing you
Was the start of me really liking you
I knew this because my feelings been hurt
On the way home I never thought why
Until I saw your beautiful brown eyes
From that moment on I had to get to know you better

So with stage 1 and 2 out of the way
Next was 3 and 4
Then eventually more
I couldn't wait
So we talked on the phone and time went faster and faster
First for a few minutes
Then almost 4 hours
Conversations went so smooth you knew what I liked and I knew what u liked too
The conversations turned us into best of friends

So stage 5 had to begin
I wrote you some letters
You wrote some back
In these we expressed how we felt
When we couldn't act them out
This is the day I was waiting for when I can come home and see your beautiful face

My Name Is

The man
David Spence
Is just a man
With three names
Two given
One adopted into
So I can be found
The government needs to keep track of me
Three names
Many titles
With more to come
Like
Brother
Son
Grandson
Uncle
My family gave these to me
As I gave these to others
Best friend
Boyfriend
Husband
"Still no wife"
Titles of affection
Not to be confused with who I am
So I am nothing but a man
It is you
You who make me
You who make me
You who make me who I am

David Spence
A man

Mom'ma Rose

Why you're here for me I really don't know
Things were done since I've arrived, and yet you're not gone
Confusion fills my head
With words to express
My love
My thanks for all you've done
Just for being there
Even though I'm not your son
With words of encouragement, and tough hard decisions
You got me through, and now I can reach out to you
Six months ago I barely knew your name
But nine days later I felt I knew you for at least half my days
You came in so quickly
You and your kids
Why you trust me so
It confuses my brain
But for you
You should receive all of my love
Respect, kindness and all
All I have to offer hopefully to my future in-law
So thanks for taking me in and treating me like a son
And for being my shoulder while my other was gone
To you who went out on a limb for me more than once
For you who help and I almost ruined your life
Forgive me if you can
But I love you like my mother
And my aunt
You play the role of two
But just for title sake your also my mother too

Hungry 4 Knowledge

I plan to steal
Steal information
They've tried to long to keep me in the dark
Had right to call me the "N" word when I was ignorant
I had to find away to educate
Make sure they could never say that to my off spring
So I plan to steal
Steal the information
No one is willing to give or sell to me
Take the information to everything that stimulates me
Even steal the things that may be of no use to me
Someone meet I should reap what I stole for free
After all that's why I'm stealing it
Information is suppose to be free
But they priced it to slow my progress
Trying to keep me from greatness
I can tell you this
No one will ever call me the "N" word again
After I steal all the information my seed will be more educated than I ever dreamed
But it starts with educating me
So I have to steal
Steal my education

Milk's Secret

Nature's original cup
Presented to help give life
To generations for years
And more to come
Caring embrace of a gentle sense of grace
Through the soft tips of provision
As lips handle the squeezing suckle
Romanced by finger tips
Playful tickles
Warm kisses
Press firmly around the love
Embedded in the fragrance
In the soft supple love
From nature's cup

Lovejones

"Deep in thought?" she asked
As I stood there gently beside her
She examined me
Up and down her eyes looking
While her friends looked on
She wanted to know what I was thinking about
So I reluctantly told her
As she ordered from the bartender
"I'm thinking about a woman I saw once"
Is what I told her
Knowing I was talking about her
My nerves caught up to me
Allowing silence to creep in
So I introduced myself
"David, David Spence"
As I extended my hand
She replied
"Lady of Sun-rise"
With a smile that made my nerves even more on edge
That's when I bumped her glass
Paid for her drink just before
She gave me some advice and walked away
So I decided to do the same
So I walked, walked up on stage and performed a poem entitled her name

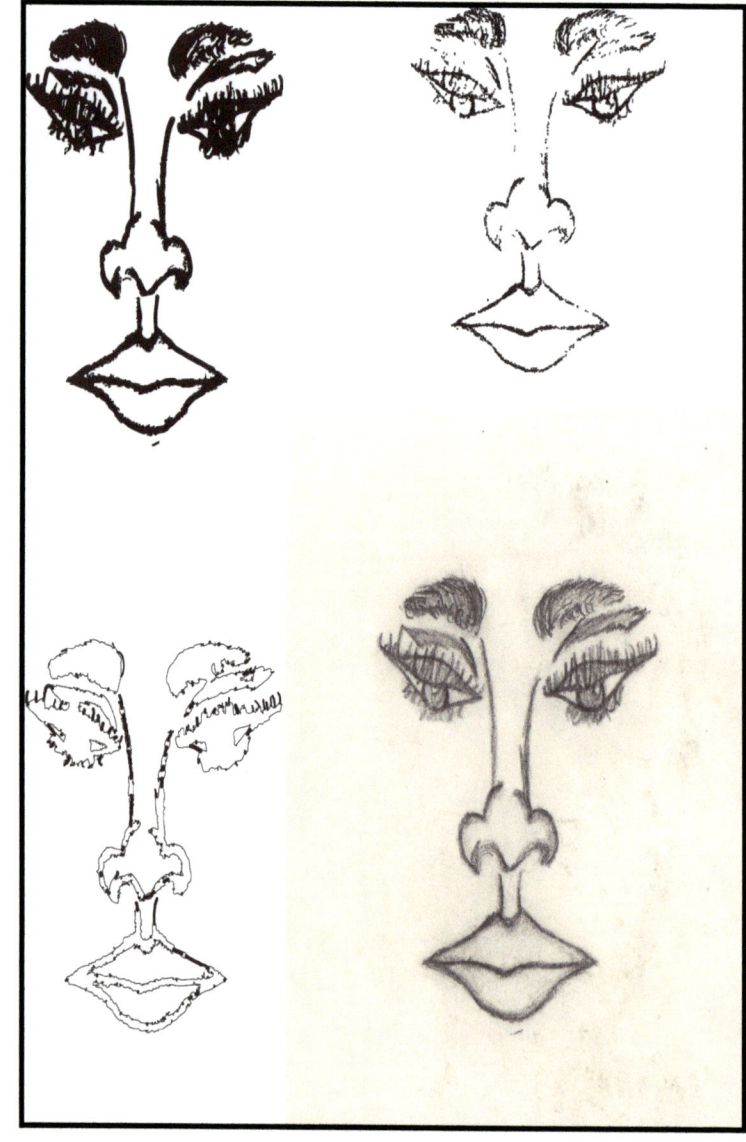

Caught By Fire In Your Eyes

Your eyes are like a fire
Shimmering in the wind
The glimmer captures my attention
And pulls me into your world
Your eyes speak to me
From the bottom of your soul
When you speak your eyes are where I go
Your body moves like a ship on a lake
The attitude and sexiness
Pulls me in like the tide during ruff winds
Each curve, is a wave
Capturing me in the domino effect of your sexual appeal
Each curve gets bigger as you come closer
Then you hit me
I see your full figure of beauty
The neck, lips, breasts and hips
Everything about you starts pulling me in you
What once started with fire
Has burned a space in my life
A mark branded by your touch
I'm now yours
Branded by your love
From the fire in your eyes

14
P.M.

Situations rising, about who I am now
I'm from T.O., born and raised in Calgary, an Albertan all the way
C.A.N.A.D.A, I'm new to this trade
Canada's free, we never had any slaves
In fact we took them away, or did we?
See that's another topic all together
So I ran for P.M.
To spark a change
3 times a charm
first round kind of close yet I pulled it off
second time, had more people backin' me, more power behind me
third time it was all me, all the ridin's mine
on fourth it should happen again
I think the people started a trend
I wasn't Jean Chretien
I was only "questions" back then
On a good day, so I tried something new and visited my fam from the NY, Brooklyn way
So I try it down here, or would my story be like the Al Gore, w. bush year
I'm not into all that counting
That's a US thing
But I crossed the boarder
So now is that my thing
I have friends who don't understand
Not feeling the US things I do
They don't understand
But that's me I'm a cultural man too
I've been through situations most would call out of hand
I've been here many times before
Something's you don't know
A political genius
Runnin' PR from the streets
I've protected my name
The one given to me
Hiding
Changing

My mentality
To keep my name strong for my moms to see
I was never about how far I would go
I'm a ladies man
No one has to know
A real, freaks-kind of freak
There's things I've done
Yo I didn't even see
Are you the type to get it out of me?
Lets cast a vote
This is a democracy
I'm doing what I need to do everyday
To please myself
My love
My ladies
So that's why I resigned
Retired from my positions
Held for so long
PM 3 times
I miss it
Could have been a fourth
But being a pimping master isn't easy my friend
No joke

16
IMPERFECTIONS

sometimes imperfections
make beauty that much more beautiful
the dimple that sits off center on your left cheek
while your right lip curls
from the shift in your tooth
and smile showing off the pearly whites
that slight extra squeeze/not fat
you get from your love handles
makes holding your waist
that much more pleasurable
especially when you laugh from my tickle
and I hear that snort when you really get into it
the angle you stand when your making eye contact
the licking of your lips when you start to smile
the simple ways you have
when you think you've done something wrong
even though you haven't
you apologize just because you are who you are
i love you
beautiful in every way that's why
what people see as imperfect makes me love you even more

Constant Attraction

As I look at another
I see pieces of you
Thinking our friendship with each other has grown
A flower in bloom
When I look at you
I begin to stumble
You make me want to fall to one knee with you
A lady which could easily steal away
the treasures I have locked away
You are the one I see myself giving my last name to
I see the women that can make me the Daddy
I should be
So as I look at another lady besides you
It's not because she's more beautiful
Or attractive to me
I look to remind myself of who I have
And why I was and still am constantly attracted to you

Ebony Kingdom
"Conception seq. #1"

Soulful Queen
Princess of my dreams
Empire of your desires
From the feelings of your aroma
My royal duty is to satisfy you
I summon my royal beast
In an attempt to please the arousal
Deep inside your womb
Clinging to this king size chamber
The generations begin to groan
Grow in attempts to moisten your ebony soil
Yearning moaning to understand you
Feel your wisdom surrounding my kingly crown
Shivering as the diamonds
From your tiara
Embraces my children in your womb
Sensual Queen
Desirable princess
Women of love

Untitled #72

It is almost your day
But we're apart
There is not much I can do to see you
But I can hear you
To send wishes
On your day
With love
But it's just wishes
Truthfully
I miss you
Not a kiss
Or a hug
But my love
I send
For even though we are not
Face-to-face
I am there while you're here
In my heart
And soul
Where my mind holds you
And tells you

Happy birthday on your special day
From you know who
To you
You know it well
So dido to you
From me
I know the same is for me to

In Love With Yourself or The Possibility?

Self pride, reasons of doubt spoken to your spirit
No one feels your worth, or that's what your eyes see
Hatred from people being used by envy
Mistrust & subconscious acts of anger towards your spirit
You have no choice, but to hold on to self-acceptance
The only time you know you won't be let down or pushed aside
But onlookers see conceit & not the lack of love giving, feeding your spirit inside
So now you ask yourself
Am I in love with myself or in love with the possibility of loving myself?

Devol

Love is 2 feel
2 understand & know
Who loves u
Who u love & whom u loved
Then there is that time
When those u love
U now devol a form of love
With misunderstandings
The times u may say
I hate u
That's all just in anger
A feeling that will pass
Devol comes and goes
Mostly u cry
Devol is real
Devol is life

The Cee-lo Green Mentality

Gone r the dayz of my innocents
Stolen away by sex and chips
It's junkfood 4 my spirit
My soul feels no end
To the pain of losing my long lost friend
Virginity I wish I kept
Not exploring the Rick James side of me
I've learned to accept
Like Visa, it's accepted everywhere
Like Amex, it's so much apart of me
I never leave home with out it
Expressing myself in American customs
Quickly moved from down south
To north eastern mentalities of the Dot
Historically followed the tongues of southerners
Use of words, actions & terms
Only made my actions more accepted by peers
Talking about hips & fingers
Shapes & figures
Designed to fit my up front agenda
To perform what is known to me as the Cee-lo Green mentality

The Bloody Page

The black ink hits the page
This usually means thoughts are being released

The release of pain flowing quickly
Violently killing the page with dramatic metaphors
Of how sick I am of the world

The release of frustration, dripping on what I find as deaf ears
Speaking about problems related to my well being
Translated into what the world expects of me

Followed quickly by CAPITALIZED letters to clearly free myself verbally on the page
I'M SICK OF SARCASTIC PSYCHO BABBLE
Insulting my life as nothing more than simple rhetoric

As my pen tears the page like flesh
Roman torture with no remorse
The pen has become an extension of me
The page a bloody image of revenge
As the black ink leaks from the imagery of frustration, on the page of my life

24 I Almost Let Go

Really you know I want you but that really just can't be
See I don't know if I can actually be with anyone until I satisfy me
Plus, I really and truly don't know if I can actually find myself getting over you
Since I loved you more than I really loved myself
Giving you the thing that you wanted
My Heart
But I never had it to give for myself
Never had it to give when you wanted me to
I honestly don't know if I love you or like you like I once did
But my love is still strong like the feeling of your body is pressing against me
Like the night when I came to visit ya
And we laid next to each other watching movies on TV
While speaking to each other silently our minds are linked emotionally
Telling each other about how much we loved each other
When we would spiritually hold hands, spiritually kiss and mix our love
Your lips pressed softly on mine as I try to release
Physically I just can't let you go, I can't let you go
I still feel my mind speaking to your soul deep in your mind
Connected deep in my heart
My left ventricle plays a part of how I see you when I walk in the dark
Thinking about our night in the park taking pictures
Reminiscing of our love
Your beauty I saw you naturally while holding you close to me
But I just can't get over you
Why can't I let you go?
Looking at ducks in the river, reminds me of dinner you made for me
The next morning we ate as I fried up some eggs
But I can't let you go
My heart still beats for you but my mind can't think of you
Cause if I do my eyes will start crying for you
That's why I don't say your name
It reminds me of the name I almost gave away and I still want to
I just can't let you go

Your Beauty Reminds Me Of

The flicker in your eyes
From the stars located inside
The fullness of your lips
So round so full
Reminds me of tulips
Your cheeks are soft like rose petals
While your neck a latter to your platinum room
Where I can see the way you see
Through the windows in your room
Let me figure out everything about you
Where to go to understand you
And how to get to your palace of gold to love you
Can I stare at the stars that I find day and night?
Will you allow me to kiss your tulips, rose petals?
With my lips
Allow me to find your palace of gold
To make it to your platinum room
Will you allow me to tell you how much your beauty reminds me of loving you?

26
Rain on Me

She hears the pitter patter sliding down her windowsill
The rain drops begin to speak to her
"Take this pain from me"
As she curls up on the bed thinking about what the night holds
Dripping outside
She reads her "Black Erotica" by Zane
Turns on her stereo to Maxwell's "a women's work"
Softly, as the pages turn
She thinks of him
Picturing him as a character in her book
She starts to breathe deeply, but anger fills her
She got a broken heart
She remembers
As a bang strikes her window
Thunder sounds
Agreeing with her pain
She looks out her window to see him
Standing out in the rain
Flowers in hand
He pleads to come in
Wet from the rain
The peddles fall to the floor as she puts down her book
He turns up the Maxwell
Who turned into Ginuwine asking what's in those jeans?
He becomes her Prince
While she changes into her purple lingerie and joins him on the balcony in the rain
As they speak to her
His lips connect to her lips
As water drips down the inside of her thighs
Speaking to her as it rains harder and harder
Soaking them together
Backs arched on the balcony rail
Hips wet, thighs parted
Just before the sun comes out
After it finished raining he says
Do you forgive me?

Spoke W/ Tongues

Not always what you do
Sometimes it's what you say
When it comes to lovin me

As we spent most of our time tied to each other
Long nights of passionate stimulation
Our tongues spoke many languages
Yet our dialects differed from another
Love & lust
Visual imagery of our conversations
Of foreplay and debates on body language
Through our connection spoke to each other
Pulling & pushing
Each other closer & closer as we spoke
Silently @ times
It was still full of passion
We used actions, words, music
To exxxpress what we felt
When we couldn't say it any other way
Passion altered what we felt
We had to say
As we spoke to each other with tongues

Not always what you do
Sometimes it's what you say
When it comes to lovin me

Don't you agree?

Trichotomy : this is me

Neo Expression

I'm a being without emotion
I said!
I'm a being without emotion
So why are you making me feel the press of anger throbbing through my vein?
The sudden beat of love pounding in my chest
The pain that comes with the fate of living with emotions
The inconsistent ups and downs of "Vivian's emotional roller coaster"
The falling pitter patter of "Jill's Love Rain"
Singing songs about guys named "Tyrone"
"Apologizing to mothers"
And everyone is saying the same "Common" phrase "I use to love her"
Now your in love all over again
Again I'm a being without emotion
I said!
I'm a being without emotion
Where hearts crack and break
Like clay on a potters wheel
In my mind the "Musiq" of this "love"
This emotion is making me crazy
Half of me wants "real love"
But the "world outside my window" is scattered with "voodoo's untitled" hits
Making me "sweat" with guitar riffs
Strumming "Jason's Lyric" only "the funk in your right thigh" is saying
I am a being of emotion
Saying
I am "ready for love"

Psyche

Id

Ego

Conscious

Sub-Conscious

Selfish

I've been messing up
I've been shying away
Misconstruing the truth
How I live
How I love
Who I love
Why I live
Why I love
It's all selfishness
To validate my faults
Positive
When positive
And negative
Is negative
My entire life a lie
My positivity as an RBG
Negativity
All caused by self-preservation
To maintain my image of acceptance
To maintain my standards
Standards I don't meet
My entire existence
A sham
A false sense of acceptance
In actuality I'm selfish
I only think of my feelings
Not accepting yours
My heart is a lie
My love is selfish
My heart is selfish
My love is a lie
I AM SELFISH

34 I Have a Dream Too

I heard your question
I'll tell you this
My first wish is that all men grow up from the mindset of boys II men
Singing songs of more than overcoming
More than when I start running
From whips of oppression, 'til my soul starts out humming
I'm no longer running but singing
About songs that state
I'm more than a conqueror, while running this race
For the race is not for the swift, but the strong
I've been strong from the date my breathe first broke the plain
So I'll make this plain
I'm more than a leader
I'm a father in the cause
Following the steps of my forefathers in this cause
Thru progress they achieved and opened up doors
With my concepts, I believe and press for more
To be like the ones who were shot down, by the weaker individuals
Whose personalities tend to follow the mentality of Judas, the deceiver
Their betrayal seemed to defeat them at the hands of their own evil
So I'll father my seed and lead them from that evil
They will grown into a leader
And lead her

35
Psyche

That Only Leaves 3

Is the deaf, really deaf?
Is the blind, really blind?
Or is it the ones who can see blind and who can hear deaf?

1. Blind to everything around them
The different cultures
Events
They let racism take over them
They have no love for who they see
Thinking always in three
With sex
Money
And myself on my mind

2. Or is it deaf that you really are
Insensitive to all that's going on
You hear about the pain
The struggles
Even those who been slaughtered
You've gone cold to what is told to you
But act in silence instead of with your head

3. You are none of the above
Sensitive to the world and its events
Ready to live according to make people feel good

So pick one or the other
Even better neither its time to
Love one and each other
Stop living for yourself
Bring strength with help

So which are you?
Choose 1, 2 or 3
As for me I'm neither 1 nor 2

Hard To Know Me

Can you understand me?
Do you know what I'm really about?
There are many parts to me
I don't even understand
Five elements and six eras that I can calculate and remember
Pieces of me that I'll let you figure out
Others that you'll probably know nothing about
When you ask I'll tell you nothing
When you search you'll find nothing
The search will end right where it started
To dig for an answer is to fall into a pit with no end
There is only one era of me that is secretive
But to be apart of me is to understand all of me
To understand era number one is to gain my trust
To gain my trust is to understand more than era number one
Who knows where my trust will lead you
I have yet to understand myself

5th Element of Hip Hop

I am the 5th element of Hip Hop
I should have been the 1st
I could even be the 2nd
I could have even been the 3rd and 4th
Other aspects of culture took authority over me
I am the voice of all nations
So I should be the 1st element of all cultures
1 I speak with emotion
2 I speak with anger raging/lust/sex/passion blazing
3 I speak with spiritual intentions of praising
I am the 5th element of Hip Hop
5th to graffiti writing
5th to deejays
5th to emcee's
5th to break dancing
I am the last element of Hip Hop
But I should have been first

I am poetry the spoken word

Artistry

He sat silently; as he watched his ideas come to life
The simple expression of his mind formed words from his thoughts
Thoughts that defined artistry for a lot of people

Words stage that which we call life
With simple expression of his mind he formed creations from his hands
His hands molded countless works of art
Works of art that inspired many replicas in his creation

He spoke with his mind
He molded with his mind
Encouraging me to do the same
Think before I speak
Think before I act
Creating and reciting masterpieces
Building artistry first in my mind

He developed perfection within seven days
I understand his perfection with in eight thousand seven hundred sixty-six days
My artistry I've developed in about the same
Artistry that strives to be like my mentor
The one who I always looked up to and who always thinks of me

In my mind where my mentor created
Created me to think
Edifying and understanding emotional creations
Molded by him
Who taught me to mold words, from my mind like him
To be a creative artist for him
That is almost like him

Could that be me?

I sit in the alley writing love letters
But I'm not in love
Never really understood love
So I guess I'm in the alley writing letters
Romantic letters maybe
Letters of lady luck
Wrapped firmly in my arms
Feeling a tender kiss
The warmth of her nipple placed firmly on my cheek
But I've never felt the warmth on my cheek
Never really understood the hype over sexuality
So I guess I'm fantasying on how it would be
The simplicity of meeting the woman of my dreams
AGAIN
I lost her, so I wonder if this time things will work out in the end
So I'm in the alley watching a couple
Wondering if that will ever be me
The irony is I've been writing replacing him with me
But I know that could never be
So I continue to write in the alley love letters to myself
Until I have someone to share them with

Disrupted

I was trying to write earlier
But was unable to
You see as I wrote, I also heard and what I heard was my name
MY NAME
What was being uttered about me?
I felt various emotions
Hurt, because of some things that were said
Truth towards other things
But over all betrayal
I was being discussed
When they felt I wasn't around
Discussed when they felt it was right
While I was trying to write
I had to leave you and focus on what was going on around me
Why me?
Is there some reason why my name was the target?
So when I couldn't take hearing no more
I LEFT!
Quickly followed by those involved
"I do not appreciate being discussed by anyone"
My response to questions uttered by them as I walked away
Trying to figure out where my head was at
And it needs to be where you are
A frame of mind that speaks knowledge, and I know why I came back

Forced2Focus

David, Out

I am a Black Man

I'm a man who loves
To see women succeed
A man who knows how to live
For the women of his dreams
I love to see our people make it
Not falling for the lies* that the white man gave them
A people where the women
Becomes stronger than before
Black women
They are stronger than all of us
A people who don't listen
To the black man's bull-shit
Living to be a success
Not a nigger like the cracker said he is
A people of black leaders
Striving to grow
And bring up the black man below
I am a black man
Looking for a black man
To teach me how to be a man
I am a black man
Searching for a black women
To teach me how to love
To love a real black woman
I was questions
A black man searching for a people
A black people to help answer
My question
Do we want to survive?

I DON'T KNOW WHAT IT'S LIKE…

I don't know what it's like to experience the things that make your life seem just oh…oh so amazing
The things that you find, somehow add extra meaning
Yet with the simplest things
Gestures, moments, times when you were not actually yourself
The time you were caught off guard
The time you went out of your way, when your way really meant less to you than that person did

I really don't know what it's like to experience the things that make your life seem just so….so unbelievably scary
That it gets your heart pumping at rates that should probably kill you
That event that usually leads up to that suspenseful music in a thriller, and you're the victim
That sudden urge to run, but your feet won't move
Or your to dumb to tell yourself to

I've never known anything like this
I've known of people like this
But it has never, ever actually happened to me

That feeling of love that suddenly rushes through you when you connect with that person you seemingly just can't forget about
No matter how much you try
That unequivocal urge that you have to be around them everyday, but you know you are unable to just because they are who they are and you
Well you are just you
This usually leads to you being someone you are not just because you long to be around whom they are no matter what sacrifices you have to make

I don't know what it's like
I've never had to experience that type of emotion
Frankly I don't actually think I really want to either
It just sounds hurtful
Sounds, sounds a little too overwhelming

The type of overwhelming that makes you forget the type of person you are
The type of person you grew up to love
The type of person you actually needed to be
Just so that you could be introduced to this feeling
A feeling that I never want to say I've experienced

So I'll just say
I don't know what it's like…I don't

In my truest form
Esskei

Emptiness (Death Part 1)

Empty shells
Vessels of my life
Void blank
No trace of hope in sight
But I see death black and grim
Approaching ever so quickly to kill
Who does he want?
Hopefully not me
Still my life is hopeless
He breathes my name
Ever so quietly
Fast approaching
Faster still
I cry out
NO!
I'm gone
It's come
Death

Against The System

The system
Holds us down
Persecuting one nation
Like strangers out of town
"We live here too"
A common cry
Along with a cry of hate
Anger and frustration
I want to die
Distance between what we think
You think we're always wrong
This, another song
No will!
No way!
Says the man with the remote
Pushing the buttons to your heart
Mind and soul
You lost yourself to the system
Bitching & complaining
Stop crying!
Stop complaining!
Stop bitching!
Try to make a difference
For your holding the system
Yourself down
From making your life what it should be
For you and your people
"Fight the powers that be"
Raise your fist
March to victory
Breaking one chain at a time
Until you set your nation free

Inter-dimensional Consciousness

We say the system holds us down
Listening to the stories of your friends
Blaming the white man for so called lies told by our fellow man
You been had, sold by your own nation
Thinking the "MAN" had done you wrong
Isn't it true, we're a nation where earth began?
So slavery must have started from the touch of our hand
But because of lies
The white man took what we owned
Is it okay that your brother turned you over for 30 pieces of gold?
A new name, family and got out of the slave trade
And you blame the "system of white men" saying
I will never get a brake
How wrong you are, living in a lie
From the system of slaves and thieves.... Nigger that is what we were called
The white man called us this, while our black man did us wrong
We're all slaves who have been freed from our chains
But many turn to leave and find yet stronger binds of chains
Holding them down in there mind, mental slavery from our own kind
The "MAN'S" not holding us back, they freed us a while ago
It's us who don't want to see each other succeed
Placing chains in this mental slavery
Why? Cause we only worry about ourselves
In this so called set back by the "MAN"
We think this way because we're stuck in between two truths
The consciences of the truth and the lies feed to us since birth
Can we learn to take responsibility for the lies?
Told from way back when
Or will we constantly believe the system is killing us my brother
And not you and me, my friend
Trapped in between two levels of truth
We need to find one level to live on to be free
So think with your mind, about the conscience truth
And believe what will free you from mental slavery

Money Not Sense Controls Individual Intent

Only he knows
What's wrong with me?
The pain of not accomplishing exactly what was set up to be complete
Changes my make up
With a smudged foundation
Simple powder can not cover up
My faults
The blemishes that I've developed
Trying to squeeze perfection out of imperfection
Because society acknowledges cover ups as beauty
Turns my desire to remain me
Now I'm obsolete
As I look in magazines seeing images of individuals
Altered to fit the universal image of who they say I should be
The decrepit face of death
Where individuality was replaced
The power of $$$
Sex appeal, perfection and weight loss controls today's society
Taking away everyone's
True identity

New Revolutionary

Like Malcolm or Martin
I found a new understanding of self determination
So many haters around me
They made it hard to find the X
Involved with being a man of God
Outside the living waters I saw a man who claimed to be on my side
He wasn't respected locked away for crimes all hearsay
Mandela finally free
Now Marcus' name is next to be cleared so Jamaicans can call him a hero like Cubans see Che Guevara
I am the next generation of freedom fighter
In a society where, Christianity turned away from their civil responsibility
It's time for me to be persecuted until the people see the truth
And thank God for opening my mind
To lift my fist and fight for you

Not a Conversationalist

I'm not an individual known for big words
That's just not me

I tend not to discuss events
Readily outside my focus
But yet still people seem to surround me
Speaking to get into this individual's head
While they speak
I watch
I listen
Trying to come to terms with my surroundings
The conversation for me flows
In my mind
And barely slips out from that focus
I know
My words seem trapped in my head
That is because they are
I don't have time for no long talking
Yuh nah see it

S~5~N

So you don't know me
But think you know me better
And don't know what my name means
In three simple figures
If you go from S~5~N and you don't know my name
Don't make up any names
Trying to go toe to toe
My name isn't simple
It means a lot
Many may have it but that's alright
For S is both middle and last of my name
5 is the first of my name
As well as the title for both first and middle
While N is the end of the middle
Holding everything together
So to know my name
You first must know my GOD
If you don't know him your whole idea is fraud
For I belong to him
So can you imagine what S~5~N means
I'm royalty
He's the King and I'm his Prince
Don't try to match wisdom or knowledge with me
The S~N has that covered
For you speak and I acknowledge your understanding
But reverse the situation
I stand alone
One group of wisdom seekers, fleecing the Lord
So try again to understand my name
S~5~N
For you don't know David Spence with out the
S~5~N

Public Transpo

If you're like me and most everyone else you say this first thing in the morning
"Can I get a transfer please?"
Right before you walk on the bus
But ain't the bus a joke
The people you see, and more important the ones you meet
When you walk on the bus
Transfer in hand, bag on shoulder
Or newspaper in briefcase, along with phone ringing early in the morning
Who in the world is calling you, when you just got out your house?
But it's happened to me too
So no complaints coming from over this way
But someone is looking my way
A beautiful young lady, no so I just smile and turn away
Ding the bus comes to a requested stop
3 people come off, but 5 to 7 more people come on
And you thought it was going to be just you in that back row
Ding another stop or so you think
It was just some kids playing one of there stupid games
I get upset because I'm already late for work
However there's a part of me finding this really funny
Cause I use to do that back in my day
Then I think whose day did I ruin and make late
Now I sorry, but ahh well too late
So I lean to the corner and pretend to crawl under my blanket
And start to fall asleep
Ding the bus stops again and startles me awake
I jump thinking it's my stop
And notice that I have 3 more stops to go
Falling asleep once again
Ding the bus stops yet again
I'm startled and get anxious thinking my stop is next
But fall asleep again
Ding the bus comes to a stop
And I notice that now I missed my stop
So I dash off out of my seat and remember to gather my stuff

The bus beings to pull away and I yell out
MAN!!! STOP THE BUS!!!
And get off hoping that tomorrow won't be the same as today was on the bus

Not Slaves, But Sons

We moved from societal control
Where government seeks to rule over us
Yet one man, of limited tongue
Arranged our release
Release we choose not to accept
Carrying with us

Heritage
 That was not our own

Traditions
That was forced upon us

Culture
 That stole from them
Made it their own
And sold it back to whom they stole it from

Routine
 We were use to the life
And just couldn't let it go

Bondage
 That held us there
We still cried out for freedom
Holding and playing with slavery

Stand Against Webster's

Live by the pen
For the colour of your skin
To protect the generations
Dying from the clips
Loaded by their peers
To use as protection
However, these youngsters changed the definition
Protection no longer applies to survival
Instead they rival
War against each other
Black on black
White on white
Racial crimes against man
Against society
Making matters worse in the homes where they live
Before long the problem spreads
Like cancer
Plaguing the nation again
All from generational trends
Changing definitions is now a cultural trend
Gay went from happy to same sex relations
While nigger once meaning ignorance; to mean black person; offensive
The changes are killing us
Keeping us from deeper understanding
They made matters so bad
We're kicking down doors again
For equal rights
And real protection
To properly effect change
We need to take stands against the cancer being injected
SO THE REEVALUATION CAN REALLY BEGIN

The Girl Next Door

She was a quiet girl

Her friends thought nothing of it
The fact that she was always
Beaten & Bruised
She lived with her mother
And asked for her Daddy

He wasn't her favorite either

Now she's 16 and the only thing she knows
Is how it feels to have daddy kiss her
Her friends show concern
For their friend
No man
She's still daddy's little girl
Running from the bruise's

Mommy gave her

They try to help
Her friends of course
They see her tears inside
From the tear below her waist
It won't heal
She's trying to escape the pain
But she has no where to go
Her friends never spoke up in time
For the friend they sometimes called baby girl
But I'll always call her

The girl next door

Viagra

The fact is that I'm impotent
From being all belligerent
In a desolate still situation
My mind shutters to think of hope
While my life is a mess
That's why I'm digging in my pockets
I'm searching for hope
'Cause right now I'm not holding it
Still I know it's there
Somewhere down deep
Hidden underneath the past I just can't let go
I'm so impotent I need a wonder drug
Something to break the cycle
"I can not perform!"
No hope for longevity
Or should I say hope gave it to me
As I forget the forgotten neglect
Hopeless ignorance
Thinking a pill can give me hope
Causes me to be more belligerent
More discussed with myself
Rummaging through my pockets
In search of hope
To end this impotent cycle of self-determination
To make it work
While my life is a mess
Somewhere deep in my pockets

Ying Ying

Ying Ying
Balance
For every good
A little evil
For every evil
A little good
Things coexist with each other
So why do we?
Fights daily
Conflicts come along yearly like taxes
Dame this!
Can we balance out just a bit?
To make my stay and yours
Peace on earth
Thanks for all you've done to help in the balance
I'm glad you're still not done
For every good action
Evil
For every evil action
Ying Ying

Good-bye Faye

She's gone
Last night when I began my journey
She was here

She's gone
I never spoke to her before I left
She would have loved to her my voice
Now she can't

She's gone
I would have loved to hear her voice
The loving tone when She said "hi my son"
She greeted me with love
But now
She's gone

She's gone
No more visits and seeing her face

She's gone
Last night she began a journey
She was here
I am here
Continuing my journey that I began last night
But my auntie
She's gone

Your sister
She's gone

Your niece
She's gone

Your daughter
She's gone

She is gone

Labels

What would my life be if it wasn't defined by labels?
And Akademic's was the main reason for living
But in a world of Pure Playaz
It's hard to think of anything else but Bob Marley music that touched my soul
Children around the globe
Listening to Rocafella Records wearing Roca Wear and Vokal
The industry of music is Universal Eckoing Hip Hop cares
When Violator from Blood Line Records are Disturbing Tha Peace
Yelling Fubu
As all J Records and Def Jam Records read
PARENTAL ADVISORY EXPLICIT CONTENT
And that's suppose to be "for us by us"
Explicit lyric's is all they have to offer
While Sean John and Death Row Records
Feel they have No Limit's their Priority Records
Losing the people that made them famous
R.I.P. to Biggie and 2 Pac
Murder I.N.C. ran through Motown
Leaving the industry at Rockport
While everyone turned Def Squad not willing to speak what they seen
Flipmode Records changed the script
When Davouci and Enyce was worn by everyone at Interscope Records
Society pointed to Mecca USA
Trying to define your Triple Five Soul not about Cash Money

Openly

Open your eyes
Take a look
Oh a look
Look at me
CRYING
Tears running down my face
Wishing they will wash away my pain
My hurt
My anger
Loss of my friend
That distinct feeling of mourning
Thought of sunrise when the moon clearly shines
LOOK AT ME
LOOK AT THE TEARS YOU CAUSED
THE PAIN
THE ANGER YOU GAVE ME
Walking in eyes wide shut
They should have been
OPEN
Open to express yourself
Your feelings at least towards me
I was suppose to be
YOURS
I was yours
You took me **my heart**
My love
And CRUSHED them between your lies
Betrayal
Adultery with another
Someone you gave
Your heart
Your soul
That never really loved
YOU
You who I loved
But love wasn't expressed
OPENLY

Psyche

Dear Daddy I love you very much I hope you are happy I love and care for you as you love and care for me. I hope you had A meery christmas and a happy mew year. Love David

Starving Art Is
[Starving Artist]

I've strived to define myself
"Hasn't anyone ever told you that you're artistic?"
Better my time
Re-invent my abilities
But the conformists reject any ideas of bettering me
The lack of understanding
To what my words mean
Why I sketched what I did
In reference to myself
Distracted me when hunger pains changed my last efforts
To re-invent myself
I fasted
Re-worked my emotions on paper
The simple pleasures I use to face
Trying only to respond to my mental stagnates
 Stressed critics who pretended to be supportive
Saying "I thought it was good"
With no real feed back or comments or concerns
I felt stifled writing for critical acceptance
Hurts to write, express and perform the concept of me
Demand by the release of expression created by the mood of me despised
By my work, my art, my personal corner
I couldn't collect my thoughts determined to reach the stage
I plugged my interests into the mixer connected to an amp
I began to project a combination of talents to the stage
My paper that I appear on day after day after day
Filling my heart with anticipation something greater is yet to come
Greater than collection of works that struggled to grab the attention of the artistic world
Lead to my studio of simple pleasures
Dim lighting and gospel music
Blend deeply and patterns and dictionaries
Cover the sheets for my creative blanket
Made neatly around a mess of pages, books
And pens consistent colours change to

Mixture of linguistic speech
To visions of shadows in pictures
That form like pillows on the bed allowing rest
For my head that change consistently daily
Full of thoughts desires to make a collection
Definitive by 1 piece of writing the raven
Edger Allan Poe Clai*ME*DeStreets
Esskei different but critically the same
Artistically searching for classification
Each time my persona reaches the
Stage that piece of paper
I appear on day after day

Youngsters Façade

Torn is the memory of the happiest days of my life
Filled with rage
My page is bludgeoned with hate
Each tear a way to inflict pain
Through a mind so upset
It made Paul Menendez seem like Elmo
Compared to what I heard you say
Releasing frustration with balled fists
As they grab the closest object
Ready to sling in repetition those objects
At the person suppose to be a mentor
Pounding back from words used to pierce deeply in my pride
Flesh bruised, damaged, connections broken
Tempers flaring as swelling began to set in
Changing the attitude of the youngster
Looking to be accepted by his peers
Empty spaces on the wall
Silence for days on end
My memories gone
Tarring apart my trust and respect for myself
Caused by the violence of balled fists and bludgeoned pages

My picture is torn
My memories erased

Pneuma

Outter Courts

Inner Courts

Holy of Holies

73 Pnuema

Dinner Skipped Me

Where do I belong?
I'm missing my place at the dinner table
Everyone forgot about me
Am I meant to wander aimlessly?
Please help me find out where I belong
Should I follow or should I lead?
Many may object to my leadership
While others don't wish for me to follow along side them
So now what do I do?
Do I go about things one-against the world?
That's too hard for me to do right now
I need more than myself to accomplish a task like that
Could I get a hand Lord?
Someone on earth to fight along side me
Or is there no one for me?
I asked you where I belong
Now I am asking
How do I survive?
To live alone
Is to die alone
While to live out of place
Is to die out of place
And I only can do this for so long
Then I'm gone
My mind can only think like this for so long

Substitute Teacher

You built the world with a simple word
The sun, moon and stars
Appeared as you waved your hand
Land and sea
Form with a bat of an eye
Then came man who took a little more love & time
For him you formed and sculpted in your image
Then breathed life everlasting
Into a man of no grounding
As you came down in the cool of day
You spoke to him and made away for him to understand
And know your laws
But he was lonely
So as he slept a rib was moved
 You took the same care as before to make his mate
And you told him to teach her your will to know all that's right
But things went missing in your teaching somewhere along the way
He understood you my Lord
But as for her and his teaching something was missed or unsaid
But life goes on from the first day of sin
Lord you came back and made things right again
But man missing a point
Things are getting worse
I just can't wait till you come and take your church

As I Pray

Lord
I thank you
For your mercies
Grace
Understanding
And honesty
My love
Can't imagine
Life without you
To wallow in
Sin
Death
Of my own filth
So
I lift my hands
To you
In
Gratitude
For the advocate
With thee
And for dying
For me
So help me
As I pray
To
Press on
And make it
Were I can be
Beside you
Lord
Who I Love
And there is
No one
Above
I thank you

Classic Salvation Sauce

Large mixing bowl "YOU" full of sin, come as you are when you come to the Lord
1 HEART full of love and forgiveness
1 Mustard Seed, you'll need this to make your faith stronger, a little does a lot
1 Bag of bottomless repentance
1 Baptism, to clean all the other ingredients
1 cup (8 oz) Spirit "The Holy Spirit"
7 "Gifts of the spirit", add each gift as you acquire them
1 whisper of the NAME of JESUS, this gives you power
1 Bible and Prayer

Step 1: Take large mixing bowl full of sin and mix them together with 1 bag of bottomless repentance. Bring to the Lord and Drain the sins from the bowl.

Step 2: Heat the Mustard Seed and mix with Baptism. Bring to a boil and pour into the large mixing bowl. Place the HEART full of love and forgiveness and stir for 3-5mins. Allow to simmer and add in the NAME of JESUS.

Step 3: Add cup of Spirit, to the mixing bowl and bring to a boil. Make sure to use all 8oz.

Step 4: Place any of the 7 gifts of the spirit to your mixing bowl. Allow the Holy Spirit to work upon you while pray and read your bible to gain your other gifts.

Step 5: Allow sauce to simmer, always adding gifts to spice up your salvation. Never let settle and always bring to a boil.

Forced 2 Focus

See my mind is here
While my heart is here
And my soul is here
Yet he hold's them all here
In his hand
He said out of your belly shall flow
But why is it that my water seems short
Is it because someone is blocking me?

Forcing me to survive off the draught which is my spirituality
Or is it the fact I might have sinned last night
And God built a damn until I repent from my heart
Or is it because my mind is stayed on him
But my heart doesn't love Jesus
My soul lives for Christ
Yet my heart and mind are un-balanced sitting on a fence
Not yet ready to swing on over to him
Or perhaps the roles are reversed
Maybe my heart loves Jesus
"Falling in love with Jesus"
But my mind isn't stayed on him
That can't be it can it?
Is that why I feel spiritually drained
Or is it because I'm being persecuted
Placed in a Jim Crow era
"The spiritual section"
Somewhere you go when everything is right but what the nature of man sees
That's when you get back benched
That's why your living waters isn't flowing as it should
But that can't be it?
There has to be more
I know there is one last thing
This the biggest reason of all
I let the devil use them to get to me
That's why
"I have to keep my mind stayed on, stayed on Jesus"
Because I learned that
"Falling in love with Jesus is the best thing I've ever done"

God 4 Give

God forgive me
For my actions/my sins & my disgrace
That I placed on your name
Thinking bout peace/love & grace
About the time you took my place
Out there/hanging on the cross
You didn't have to do it/but you did
So I thank you Lord/let's begin

They beat & bruised your good looks
Like it said in your good book
You carried the cross/and even when you couldn't make it
God you said "I have to take this"
Simon was placed in your path/with the patience
The love in you gave him the strength
To weight this
Helped you up to Calvary
Where you bleed and died for me
There's so much that I can say
But let me talk about your grace

God forgive me
For my actions/my sins & disgrace
That I placed on your name
Thinking bout peace/love & grace
About the time you took my place
Out there/hanging on the cross
You didn't have to do it/but you did
So I thank you Lord/let's begin

Hook: Change Bridge: Mentality Verse: Sin

God thank you for waking me up this morning
My mind is here now
Unfortunately it slipped last night
But I'm back now
Many people tried to create
A persona something they took from me
But other things they placed on me
Characteristics of things they wanted me to be
TOO BAD

It's harder than life it's self
When you live to please others
The success of ones self is determined from a cover
Usually parents like a mother or a father
Well when you look at me
You should see a man who loves his mother and spiritual father
But I'm tired of people labeling me
"Christian"
Take Christianity and tell me where that makes spirituality
The four walls you live in determine sin
Sorry I'm human, it's going to happen
But God does forgive
Don't get me wrong life isn't meant to fuck up
Sorry for the language
On purpose
But this world today is dying and ya'll are crying about shit
Sorry yet again
Pushing people away, you affectionately call friend
What happen to the days you was down with me to the end?
I guess the end means you backstab to end the friendship

Why are you calling out hypocrite?
Just because they came from church politics
When the world is full of so much more compared to the four walls you decided to run from

Life is easier than you made it
Now you are coping out from responsibilities of your own sin
Take charge
Stop blaming
You did your dirt
Now clean it
I'm sorry for not reppin' your authority
I see you and believe me I don't feel you
The anointing isn't moving as it's suppose to
But really who's is?
I know I'm not right when I write
But I still have to
'Cause God still speaks
Through an imperfect vessel like me and you
That's why I can't let everything get to me
I just ask him to forgive me
And move on
Really it's time for me to move on
Write
AWW write

I Still Am

I'm going back
Regardless of what others think
I know within myself "who I am"
And even though I seldom govern myself accordingly
I still am who I've always been
I can't let the stares
The whispering
The corruption that pollutes the world
That filtered in the church
Pollute my spirit with hurt
Forcing me to leave
Because I'm not
Regardless of what others think
I still am a child of God
He may not like some of my choices
I don't either
But he loves me because I still seek him and his forgiveness
So when I walk back in
I won't let the whispering
I won't let the eyes
I won't let the questions
Change my praise
Because regardless of what others think
I STILL AM SAVED

Love @ Birth
(Dedicated to my mother)

You had me in the morning before noon
The words in my name right,
The arrangement a misfortune
You changed them around and mostly my life
It started off so small, and soon became greater
Love and kindness formed me
I then began to wait on people
It doesn't look like much but you supported me 100%
In everything I did you made sure I did my best
I came and then I was gone
A life not wasted because of you and GOD
Thank you for showing me who GOD was to you
And who GOD could be for me
I took all that and with others he was half of me
My Lord and King, GOD is to me
You on the other hand my mommy
I use lower case "m" because you're more than just mom to me
You're an advisor, a counselor and also my friend
I come to you like no one else before
I'm glad GOD
Gave you me
And I'm glad
GOD
Gave me you
Thank you
For many years
Of even more
Excellent
Wisdom
Guidance and
So much more

SHE Wondered

SHE used to come over a lot. I mean **SHE** use to talk every now and then, laugh whenever a joke was told but **SHE** would be the first to stop smiling

* I always **WONDERED** why she was so quiet only speaking when someone's comments were directed to her. To me it looked like there was something bothering her, something deep inside. The look on her face showed me pain in her eyes*

SHE used to come over a lot. I mean **SHE** use to talk every now and then, laugh whenever a joke was told but **SHE** would be the first to stop smiling

* I would look at her and **WONDER**. Why she was being so strong, holding in the pain that I seen in her eyes yesterday so I asked her what's wrong today? **SHE** said "nothing I'm alright, are you okay?"*

SHE used to come over a lot. I mean **SHE** use to talk every now and then, laugh whenever a joke was told but **SHE** would be the first to stop smiling

* I mean **SHE** used to sit down beside me. Every time **SHE** was near by but every time I looked at her I would see the pain in her eyes. That hurt that **SHE** was holding deep down inside. The emotional damage must have built up from over the years*

SHE used to come over a lot. I mean **SHE** use to talk every now and then, laugh whenever a joke was told but **SHE** would be the first to stop smiling

* This day **SHE** sat down beside me I needed to know what was wrong. I looked in her eyes and said "Why are you acting so strong"? I think
SHE needs someone to be her pot. You know someone to listen, help hold her problems so **SHE** could boil off steam*

SHE used to come over a lot. I mean **SHE** use to talk every now and then, laugh whenever a joke was told but **SHE** would be the first to stop smiling

* I wanted to help her. I wanted to be her pot. So again I asked her "What's wrong"? **SHE** said "nothing is wrong with me, how are you doing"? Me, I'm not hurt. I felt the pain from your eyes. I wasn't focusing on myself. But you are asking me if I'm okay*

SHE used to come over a lot.

* This day **SHE** sat down beside me as **SHE** asked me what's wrong. I mean the day before what **SHE** said is still a part of me. But I was looking at the hurt in her eyes. Her eyes are where I felt the pain. **SHE** said "The pain I felt is the pain within me." The pain I saw is the pain in me. Then **SHE** held my hand and prayed for me. I cried and asked God to heal me. While I thanked him for her who sat next to me and **WONDERED** why*

SHE used to come over a lot. I mean **SHE** use to talk every now and then, laugh whenever a joke was told but **SHE** would be the first to stop smiling

Our Vow

Since we've met, our worlds haven't been the same
We've laughed
Cried
Fought
And danced
Experienced emotions
No one has
You've become my universe
And I your world
You are my sun in the day
I your moon at night
You gave me peace
When I had no peace
You are a joy to behold
Each time I see you
Like a single red rose in a garden of weeds
My heart rages full of emotion
My mind fills with thoughts of memories past
I was a falling star
Shaken from my universe
But your hand caught me
Pulled me
Anchored me in your heart
So with his love
I give you mine
With his grace
I apply my patience
With his understanding
I'll be forgiving
With his mercy
I'll continually love you
For you are the love God created for me
This is our vow

So That I See You Tomorrow

Thank you Father for your blessings this day
Your love is so precious
I just don't know what to say
You were there for me when neither father nor mother would show
So I thank you for raising me, as you wanted me to grow
Thank you for the gifts given
And even more praise I give to you for the gifts that I see
Help me to find the gifts inside me
I know not
But more importantly help me to use and retain accordingly
What you have given me properly
Thank you Lord in a whole for waking me up this day
A day full of beauty and love
I pray a day like this I will see again
For my health and my strength
I bless you
For my down times
When I'm in a pit I know you will be there
To lift me up to where you want me to be
For after being down I only can go up
As my praise goes up to you
I give my heart too
Yet Lord
Many a day I've seen like this I just hope tomorrow will be the same
I love you
Amen

Time
(In Loving Memory of Grandma)

Time is of the essence
Ur time is important 2 me
After all the time u put in2 me
It's more than I believed in me

The time is deceived from what I seen
Time 2 perceive
24 hrs not enough in a day
2 praise u
4 all the things u've given me

Opened my eyes 2 more than just the clock of my life on the wall of my heart
The watch on my wrist ticking
Deeply through my pulse
When time 2 u doesn't really exist

Yet u created time 4 me 2 know when time was vast
Explained 2 me ur love
Suffered 4 hrs with our cross the weight of my sins
Time and place became dark, as u died 4 me
I counted my tears
Sorrowful 4 what grief I caused u
As I was thinking of u
Laying in that hallow tomb
I felt my tears being whipped clean
U rose
3 days later
2 comfort me
Giving me another chance at life
With time 2 spare

Thinking of You

Truly love is blind,
When I had you, feelings of joy allowed me to lose you
Now you're gone and I felt some pain
But slowly the pain began to fade
However, the love I have never disappeared
So my pride kept me away
You were my first true love
And could have been my only
This is why since the last time we spoke, I never spoke to another
Feeling my love grow once more
Like a flower in spring, during the signs of rain
The tears you cried GOD allowed to touch my soul
Only you didn't know that my eyes cried dry tears
As my soul flooded from hurt that, I caused upon myself
I now look to the love growing inside
Like the flower in spring
Flower nurtured by a caring and gentle hand
Hands I searched for, found, lost and pray for back
All this I found in you
And love you
I truly do

A New Moon

I sit on a blue moon
Wishing it would turn to blood
Making that blue moon
A new moon
Shortening time
So my savior could come
The fact is I wanna be judged
Prevent me from committing any more wrong
Twisted by flesh
It condemns my spirit
Now my soul feels no rest
Unless
I take this dollar
Make change
Allow my spirit to control this flesh
Giving my soul eternal rest
With endless possibilities to rise in the end
Or end up facing my judgment
You see no more day of atonement
Instead white throne judgment
With four horse men
Bringing down fire from
HEAVEN
Heaven is my home
Where "Platinum Rooms" and kingdoms of Gold
Where all wish to go
But many won't even see the gate
See their reaching out with your right hand
While Mondex controls your chance to make change
Implanted in your frontal lob
The power to destroy your spirit
You tried to communicate to him through Motorola
But Motorola scrambled the signal
What was holy thought of
Was screaming secular messages in his name
I'm longing to be judged
Why

'Cause now everyone is Religious
Crying on the Lord to come save them
LORD SAVE ME!
Sitting beside satan
Smoking
Making their beds in hell
Waiting for the sound of a trumpet
A sound that they will never hear
Why?
Their signals are crossed
Revelations skipped
All because they only believed in part
Reading their bible
The same scriptures they did
When they meet you
Psalm 23
"The Lord is my Sheppard I shall not want
He makes me to lie down in green pastures;
He leads me beside the still waters
He restores my soul"
While I read about a man with a two edged sword
Coming out of his mouth
And nail prints in his hands
Feet
Walking in sand
As memories flash back
Images of him drawing lines in the sand
Edifying them
Who condemn
Those opposite his stand
Still
He fought back in the depth of hell
Controlling
Death
Controlling
Life
Controlling
The keys
That ultimately controls your spirit
I'm looking for the moon to change
The ground to shake

Dead to rise
The living to vanish
Putting on new appearances
Abandoning old images
Waiting to be judged
That's when I'll conform
Come to the Lord
To form me
Right before I hear
"Well done my good and faithful servant"
Making me ruler over many
I watch those conform
All conform
To growing agony
Fire consumption
Of flesh never burning
Scorching
Searing
Pain
Desperately searching for relief
That is in Jesus who is in me
I long to be judged
Sitting on a blue moon
Waiting for the day
I'm welcomed into his gates
The day that blue moon
Turns into blood
Making that blue moon
A new moon
Making me and Jesus
Jesus and I
One
"Saul" said
"Yet I desire to live"
When that blue moon turns to blood
Just before my savior comes to judge

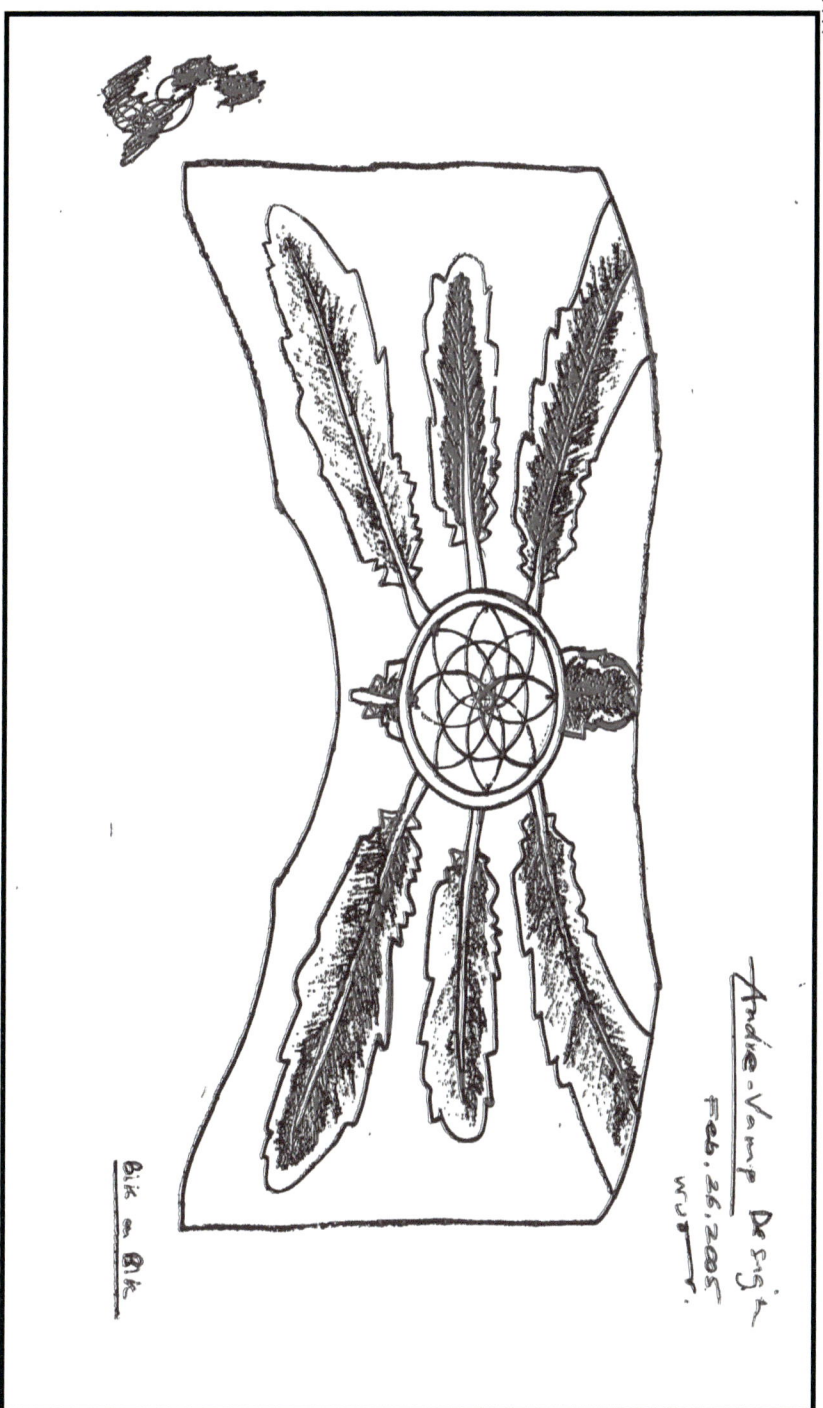

The Road to Peter
(aka a long walk)

I think about myself
The life that I was dealt
In my hands I held my wealth
The fortune 500 I expected 4 myself
But I never deserved it
The work I didn't put in
Being an entrapoor spiritual
I never saw myself working from the floor up
YOU KNOW!!
Praying never ceasing
Always keeping
Keeping my mind stayed on him
The greatest thing…
I mean the greatest one to me
He is the all mighty
Still I can't see myself…
Myself putting down work to help build his…
I'M NOT AT THE TOP!!!
But his church was built from the rock
Moulded after him
He's SOLID…
Strong like my personality to better myself
I am his son
Maybe I got it from him
Who knows?
He knows
Actually he knows all
He even knew why my company fell
I was looking in myself
Not into what he saw
My eyes can't see what I believed
But his eyes are mine
So what should I see?
If he is my eyes
Why not see my belief
I mean his vision for me

THAT'S IT HIS VISION 4 ME
I can't believe I couldn't see it
But then again I wasn't looking
Looking spiritually
My eyes were blind
Like the stars in the city
You can't see them no more
I remember when I was younger sitting in my room seeing the stars
The older I grew the more I knew
Unfortunately the less stars I seen
Pollution crept in
I never seen the smoke
Waste
Sewage
Blocking my viewage
If I only knew so much sooner
Sin wouldn't have influenced me so much
Now I feel like a looser
I was blind
But now I can see
Due to sin I still can't see the stars
I need to clean up myself first
YOU KNOW!!
Get out of myself
And into his self
See me how he sees me
Build up from the bottom up, or…
Wherever he needs me
See it's no longer about me
GLORY
Help build on the rock
Cause I live on the rock
This is the rock that I believe
But since I'm not blind
Now I can see what I believe
BELIEVE ME!!

Knocks Deception

When you only thought things would get better
The door, evil presents it's self
Proposing simultaneous knocks of sin
Corruption paces beyond the doorway begging to come in
Lurking to see which steps you'll take
Attempting to unearth your footing
To disrupt your understanding
And hide the fact it's trying to destroy your tree
Bearing fruit, producing truth
Replanting gifts
Evidence you have succeeded
Gained experience
Temptation arrives stronger
Persuasion wrapping around your seed
To strangle your future
Your ground still unearthed
Crushing generations from growing strong firm roots
Traditions
Understanding of good up bringing of solid biblical teachings
From the beginning, 'till the end is revealed
Revelations, dictated the embracing hiss of lying lips
Crawling around beyond the doorway
Peering through windows
Looking to steal my heritage
Answering the knock makes me ignorant
Inconsistent, inadequate
Disgusting isn't it?

Crucified

I need to scream
I want to cry
And run far away
To just curl up and hide
Hide from the hurt
And the pain inside
See, I always thought

"LOVE IS STRONGER THAN PRIDE"

But PRIDE it tends to get in the way
You see, it's not suppose to be about me
Then again, it is my life that I'm living

I CAN'T STAND THIS CONTINUOUS CIRCLE!!

Only living, to gain some kind of experience
I need to scream
But I can't let one out
I want to cry
But my tears just won't fall
There is nothing I'm running away from
That has hurt me but myself
I'm not in the circle
I'm on the outside looking in
Looking at the pain inside
My inconsistent achievements
"I thought I made it"

"LOVE IS SUPPOSE TO CONQUER ALL"

But running from my hurt
Only made my hurt stronger
See, I curled up for so long
Hiding from my hurt, protecting my heart from pain
That increased my pain
Instead of allowing myself to heal

100
"I CAN'T STAND THIS"

The hurt is so great
The pain is weighting me down
JESUS how in the world did you do it?
How did you allow the weight of the world to sit on your shoulders?
I can't stomach this pain
I want to scream
Because I have already cried
The night I saw JESUS hanging on the cross

This Year Christmas Made Me Nervous

The night was long
As I anticipated your arrival
The seal broken
On the bottle of olive oil
As water drips down your mother's thighs
You are on the way

Christmas is on its way
Midwives listen to heart beats
Kicking feet
Telling us you're still there
Generating smiles in between contractions
Shortening time
And nervous reactions
Quicken the arrival time
Quicken heart beats & breathing
My nerves start jittering
Looking
Holding
Waiting
You are on your way
Our first baby
Ending off the year
This is my favorite Christmas ever
However, as the hours go on
My fears begin to grow
Our first baby's approach has slowed
36 hours and he's still not here
Medical relief used to quicken his release
All in vain
Cut the waist of your mother to ensure your safety
Holding her close, I looked over
My weak stomach strengthened when I saw you head appear
No breathing
Our son was tangled by the cord meant to give him life

102

Not once but twice
My heart stopped beating at the sound of the doctor's voice saying
"He's not breathing"
Had me praying
Asking God to make sure his life remains
I wanna hold him in my hands
Hear him laugh
Do everything that I can to protect him
So this was my prayer
"Father, I know you can heal
Because you were the one who healed me
When asthma called saying he's going to take my life
You Lord turned around and protected me
Right now my son can not breathe
And my heart will not beat
I need you to open up his lungs
So that I can give you back my heart
I love you, but if you take him
I will take my heart"
It was then I heard you cry
My eyes remained dry
But my body started shaking inside
As my nerves started to subside
My heart gave way to the man that saved me and my son on the same day

I love you bum-bum

THIS IS ME!

Listening to an instrumental the music slows my thinking
The baby powder incense fills the room as I sit and focus on my breathing
I am counting to ten
I hear silence from the apartment floor hallway as my unit screams for company
I am alone
The beeping "dinga, dinga" and "there's a phone in your pocket, I'm on vibrate" sounds
My phone is ringing
Hundreds of people have access to me
Yet I feel lonely
So I answer
My phone rings with messages text to me
Verbal conversations no longer the norm
"How are you doing?" they ask
My responses so general, so no one knows how I feel
Stressed, lonely, less than perfect
Yet no one less than me would like anything to do with me
So I fill my loneliness with empty sexual encounters
I guess f'ing around is the most I'll get out of this world
And that thought alone makes me feel lonely
As my phone rings again, and another message to fill my void comes in
I ignore it and count to ten
My legs crossed, my shirt off to expose my art
My back straight and hands open ready to receive
I sit on my balcony
The city sounds fill the air
The wind blowing, kids screaming as they play, the sirens sounding from the fire station down the street
The railway crossing sounds, a train is quickly approaching
My eyes open
I hear my son
"Daddy, can I see the train?"
I look around hoping that I wasn't dreaming
He's not here

Bonus Poem

Oh I wish he was here
We'd watch the train together
So I close my eyes and I focused on my breathing
I am counting to ten
My phone rings
I answer and I hear "Hi Daddy! What you doing?"
My face lights up to reflect how my heart feels
My response
"I'm thinking of you bum bum, I'm thinking of you"

www.ingramcontent.com/pod-product-compliance
Lightning Source LLC
Chambersburg PA
CBHW041616220426
43671CB00001B/9